A souvenir guide

Cliveden

Buckinghamshire

National Trust

Built out of Love

The Duke of Buckingham chose a glorious site on the high wooded slopes above the River Thames to build a great house for his mistress in the late 1660s. Cliveden, commanding wide views over the river and beyond, has since been the home of the wealthy and titled, attracted by its favoured position and historical associations.

For more than 300 years Cliveden was home to dukes, earls, viscounts and, for a while, Frederick, Prince of Wales. Three houses have been built on this site since George Villiers, Duke of Buckingham, hired architect William Winde to design his mansion.

Winde built a great platform as a foundation, with a vast arcaded terrace giving access to the ground floor. This stroke of genius provided the base for each of the following houses.

Orkney's grand plan

If Buckingham's terrace gave the design blueprint for Cliveden, it was the next owner, George Hamilton, Earl of Orkney (1666–1737), who gave us the garden layout largely as it is seen today. Lord Orkney planned buildings, walks and woodlands, laying out a pleasure ground for his family and guests.

Cliveden burnt down in 1795 and it was left to the next owner, Sir George Warrender MP

Far left George Villiers, 2nd Duke of Buckingham (1628–87); by Isaac Beckett

Left The Duke's mistress Anna Brudenell (1642–1702), Countess of Shrewsbury, for whom he is thought to have built Cliveden; by Sir Peter Lely

Opposite Cliveden commands fine views and is a sight to be seen

(1782–1849), with his architect William Burn, to rebuild. On Warrender's death, Cliveden was bought by the Sutherlands as a retreat for Harriet, Duchess of Sutherland (1805–68), Mistress of the Robes and friend to Queen Victoria. Within six months of the purchase, Cliveden caught fire again. Queen Victoria apparently saw the smoke from Windsor and sent fire engines from the castle, but they arrived too late. Architect Charles Barry was commissioned to redesign and rebuild the house and his is the mansion you see today.

The Astors' legacy

Cliveden was owned by the Sutherlands and then their relatives, the Westminster family, until 1893, when American anglophile William Waldorf Astor (1848–1919) bought the estate, bringing with him an immense collection of classical paintings and sculpture. In 1906 William Astor moved to Hever Castle in Kent, generously handing Cliveden to his son and daughter-in-law, Waldorf and Nancy, as a wedding present.

Cliveden entered a new and glittering era, serving as a glamorous and inspiring backdrop to the parties hosted by the Astors. They were both social reformers and inveterate entertainers, influential members of the interwar intelligentsia and of Parliament (Nancy was the country's first female MP to take her seat). Their time at Cliveden saw it become one of the centres of European political and literary life.

A glamorous garden

On such a wonderfully elevated site with such outstanding views, Cliveden's garden was destined to be a cut above the rest. Lord Orkney laid the garden out, the Sutherlands beautified it, but it was the Astors who made Cliveden very grand indeed.

Little is known of the garden at Cliveden in the Duke of Buckingham's time. Contemporary diarist and gardener John Evelyn mentions an 'avenue' and 'gardens' but comments that the land was 'barren', producing nothing but 'ferne'.

It was Lord Orkney who planned and developed the garden for at least 30 years until his death in 1737. Letters to his brother reveal his progress, telling of his 'Quaker parter' (parterre) and his working relationship with garden designer Charles Bridgeman. The Ilex Grove, the Amphitheatre, Blenheim Pavilion,

Octagon Temple and the miles of walks and viewing points over the Thames were all commissioned by Lord Orkney.

Designed for a duchess

If Lord Orkney created the structure of the garden, the Sutherlands made it beautiful. Harriet, Duchess of Sutherland, in whose name Cliveden was bought in 1849, was the granddaughter of the famously stylish Georgiana, Duchess of Devonshire. Perhaps inheriting some of her grandmother's flair, Harriet worked with Head Gardener John Fleming to achieve Cliveden's innovative and elaborate planting schemes. Fleming was the celebrity gardener of his day, creating extraordinary effects with his 'ribbon bedding' and what came to be called 'carpet bedding'. This last term was coined by the *Gardeners' Chronicle*, reporting on his great circular bed of

Above Cliveden from the south in the mid-18th century, showing the Parterre and Lord Orkney's Octagon Temple

spiky echeverias and sempervivum, planted to represent the Duchess's monogram but looking as soft and well-woven as the finest carpet.

It was Fleming who devised the iconic Parterre planting, transforming Lord Orkney's plain design into the most talked-about garden feature of the mid-19th century. Today's visitors can stand on the terrace and enjoy the spectacular sight of the 16 huge beds filled with thousands of colourful plants, based on Fleming's original 1850s planting.

The Astors' additions

William Astor, son of the hugely wealthy American John Jacob Astor, settled at Cliveden in 1893. He may have been reclusive but he devoted his considerable energies to creating

Right Harriet, Duchess of Sutherland; painted by Franz Winterhalter in 1849, the year the Sutherlands bought Cliveden

Above right Nancy Astor; by John Singer Sargent

garden features in keeping with his love of the classical, in particular the Roman, aesthetic. An Italian garden (now known as the War Memorial Garden), the Borghese Balustrade, the Long Garden, the Maze, the genesis of the Water Garden and the redesign of the Octagon Temple into a family chapel all came from him.

In 1906 William Astor gave Cliveden to his son Waldorf (1879–1952) and new bride Nancy (1879–1964). The couple planted many trees and asked leading garden designer Norah Lindsay to design herbaceous borders. In time their son William, the 3rd Lord Astor, employed Geoffrey Jellicoe to design the Rose Garden (now known as the Secret Garden) and planted rhododendrons along many of the rides.

The National Trust took over the gardens in 1966, enlarging the Water Garden, replanting trees, restoring the rides, returning Fleming's designs to the Parterre and, in 2011, re-creating William Astor's maze.

The redoubtable Duchess

Harriet, Duchess of Sutherland, was a force to be reckoned with. A close friend of William Gladstone, she introduced the Italian revolutionary Giuseppe Garibaldi to London society, while organising a petition from the women of England in support of the abolition of slavery.

A Turn about the Garden

From woodland walks, beautiful riverside paths and spectacular seasonal bedding, to quiet corners for contemplation and a maze to lose yourself in, the gardens today offer as much interest as they have done for more than 300 years.

The Fountain of Love

When his father died in 1890, William Astor became America's richest man. He moved to this country in 1891, and became part of British nobility when he was granted the titles of 1st Lord Astor in 1916 and 1st Viscount Astor in 1917. His great wealth and undemanding position in the 1880s as American Minister to Italy had allowed him to indulge in his passion for European art and sculpture. So when he bought Cliveden in 1893 for £1,250,000, he brought many of the art works he had acquired to the estate. William Astor also commissioned pieces for his new home, including the spectacular Fountain of Love (1897), which stands sentinel to the House at the head of the Grand Avenue.

William Astor had practised sculpture in Rome under the guidance of fellow American, William Wetmore Story. His son, Thomas Waldo, created Cliveden's neo-Baroque fountain, its base a shell carved from three pieces of Siena marble, supporting three figures, overjoyed to have discovered the powerful elixir flowing from the Fountain of Love.

The fountain, placed in the most prominent position on the approach to the House, also marks the end of a designed vista. To the west, along a grassy ride known as Queen Anne's Walk, you can see a large sculpted urn, said to have been given to the Earl of Orkney in the early 18th century by the sovereign herself.

Before the fountain
The *rond-point*, where the fountain now stands, was previously occupied by a massive sculpture of the 2nd Duke of Sutherland, by Matthew Noble. This piece now stands at the Duke's Seat, in the woods and is visible from the terrace.

The Long Garden

This aptly named garden, filled with the formality of topiary, sculpture and bedding contrasting with informal herbaceous and shrub planting, is a striking spectacle.

In 1896, William Astor was looking for a suitable area to display some of his classical sculpture and ancient Egyptian granite baboons. Inspired by the gardens of Italy, he created narrow box-lined beds filled with herbaceous plants. The boundary wall played host to prolific climbing plants, while the southern edge was planted with shrubs. The beds ran, unbroken, from east to west, with a path in between.

His son Waldorf Astor and daughter-in-law Nancy, the 2nd Lord and Lady Astor, modified the design to create four enclosed beds, separated by a large central space containing yew topiary. Four 18th-century stone characters from the *Commedia dell' Arte* – Beatrice, Pantalone, Columbina and Arlecchino – mark the corners of the box beds. A curving stone seat rests against the wall facing the inscrutable baboons across the grassy space.

Two striking marble figures, the female Nautica, symbolising navigation, and the male, possibly a representation of Marco Polo, stand either side of the eastern entrance.

An article in the July 1930 edition of *Country Life* refers to the Long Garden as 'the main herbaceous garden', the writer praising it as 'a most charming setting for groups of herbaceous plants'.

Norah and Nancy

In Waldorf and Nancy Astor's day, the planting was flamboyant and perennial. Nancy worked closely with Norah Lindsay, their garden advisor, to devise schemes both for the beds and the wall. Today the beds are filled with colourful displays of spring bulbs and summer bedding, which change from year to year. The border below the wall is bright with clumps of perennials: geraniums, kniphofia, salvia, fuchsia, penstemons and echinacea.

and phlox, to draw the eye to the distant end of the garden.

The topiary is bold and suitably sculptural, with representations of birds in the centre and precisely clipped geometric shapes. A shrub border is being re-established along the southern edge, parallel to Queen Anne's Walk.

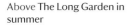
Above The Long Garden in summer

Left Socialite turned gardener Norah Lyndsay

Above right Between 2,000 and 2,500 years old, the baboons represent the Egyptian god of writing and wisdom, Thoth

Right Massed pink and deep purple tulips in a spring display

This differs from Norah Lindsay's inter-war plantings, where the quiet blue-greys of lavender and rosemary, interspersed with groups of Madonna lilies, underlined the clematis-clad wall. She planned the enclosed beds so that, seen from the east, bright colours – reds, yellows, the orange and purple of helenium, monarda, lupin and achillea – grew stronger up to and around the central point, gradually fading to greys, pinks, creams and mauves of delphinium, senecio, erigeron

The Blenheim Pavilion

George Hamilton, Earl of Orkney, planned his gardens at Cliveden with the fervour of the military campaigner that he was. A distinguished soldier, he had been second-in-command to the Duke of Marlborough at the Battle of Blenheim, in which the hitherto invincible French army of Louis XIV was defeated.

It was to commemorate this victory in the War of the Spanish Succession that he commissioned the Italian architect Giacomo Leoni to build a garden pavilion, linking the building with woodland walks planned by designer Charles Bridgeman.

Right The Blenheim Pavilion

Below George Hamilton, Earl of Orkney; by Jacobus Houbraken

A fashionable designer

Architect Giacomo Leoni was employed to design many British country houses, notably Lyme Park in Cheshire and Clandon Park, Surrey, in the fashionable Palladian style that he softened to suit owners. Lord Orkney consulted him on improvements to the house and, in addition to the Blenheim Pavilion, he asked him to design the Octagon Temple (see page 15).

The gently sloping lawn in front of the Blenheim Pavilion is a wild flower meadow and in spring is carpeted with daffodils. From the steps of the Pavilion there is a view through the woods to the River Thames. The grassy ride now known as Queen Anne's Walk was referred to by Lord Orkney as the 'Gladiator Walk' giving, as it did then, a view of his Borghese gladiator statue at the head of the Grand Avenue.

The classical stone-built Pavilion, created about 1727 as a shelter and sitting area, has a rounded arched opening decorated with slightly projecting Ionic columns flanked by single-storied wings. Carved garlands loop above the arch, while the crowning pediment bears martial carvings.

The Ilex Grove and Secret Garden

Below 'The Wounded Amazon' by William Astor, sculpted during his time in Rome in 1870, now in the Secret Garden

Formal wilderness gardens with secluded woodland walks were all the rage in the early 18th century. This is what Lord Orkney asked his designer, Charles Bridgeman, to plan in the 'Upper Gardens' in about 10 acres (4 hectares) in the north-west of the estate.

The walks, laid out at around the same time as the Blenheim Pavilion in the 1720s and encompassing what is now called the Ilex Grove, led to two clearings, known as 'cabinets', in the north and south of the area. The 'north cabinet' has disappeared but the other is now known as the Secret Garden.

Today the Ilex Grove is dominated by holm oak (*Quercus ilex*), sweet chestnut and yew, planted in the late 18th century.

The Secret Garden was conceived as a rose garden by influential landscape architect Geoffrey Jellicoe. Inspired by Paul Klee's abstract painting *The Fruit* (1932), Jellicoe wanted to express freedom and fluidity. In the 1960s plantsman Graham Stuart Thomas developed Jellicoe's concepts into detailed planting plans for the 3rd Lord Astor.

The roses eventually declined and in 2002 the Secret Garden was replanted with swathes of perennials, herbs and grasses under the direction of Isabelle van Groeningen. It still contains five wooden arches designed by Jellicoe specifically for Cliveden, three Bawden seats and a collection of sculpture, including 'The Wounded Amazon', the only piece known to have been carved by William Astor. It is dated 1870 and was perhaps carved under the direction of William Wetmore Story (see page 7) whilst William Astor was living in Rome.

In 2012 the National Trust began a project to restore the Rose Garden to Jellicoe's designs.

The Amphitheatre

This circular space, with its turf seats and views of the River Thames below and countryside beyond, was designed for musical and dramatic entertainments.

Little survives in the way of written plans made by Lord Orkney's designer Charles Bridgeman. However, we know that the grass amphitheatre carved out of the hillside at the northern end of the garden, on the slope below the Blenheim Pavilion, was probably created in the decade between 1725 and 1735, after plans for a more elaborate amphitheatre below the terrace had come to nothing.

Lord Orkney's wife, Elizabeth Villiers, a former mistress of William III, kept her contacts at court and both George I and George II paid visits to Cliveden. When Lord Orkney died in 1737, the house and estate was let to George II's son, Frederick, the Prince of Wales, as a retreat from court for him and his young family. On 1 August 1740 he invited guests to a fête at Cliveden to celebrate the birthday of his daughter, the Princess Augusta, and to commemorate the accession of the House of Hanover. The entertainment, held in the Amphitheatre, included the first performances of two masques (a form of festive courtly entertainment), with music by Thomas Arne. The first was *The Judgement of Paris*, but it was the second, *The Masque of Alfred*, with its unforgettable ending, the heroic song 'Rule, Britannia!', that fired the imagination of the 18th-century audience.

Above The Amphitheatre was the scene of the very first public rendition of 'Rule, Britannia!'

Canning's View

Lord Orkney laid out several walks along the slope to provide dramatic glimpses of the Thames. Subsequent owners maintained the paths so they could continue to enjoy these reveals of the river, and perhaps the best of all is Canning's View.

After Lord Orkney's death, Cliveden was passed down through the female line of his family until it was inherited by his great-grand-daughter, Mary in 1790. Mary was the third Countess of Orkney to hold the earldom in her own right, which is thought to be the only instance of an earldom passing through the female line for three successive generations. The countesses of Orkney lived at nearby Taplow Court, letting

Cliveden first to Frederick, Prince of Wales and subsequently to others, including Warren Hastings and John Symmons.

In 1795 fire devastated the House. Thirty years later it was rebuilt by George Warrender and began to receive distinguished visitors once more. One such visitor was George Canning (1770–1827), Foreign Secretary and, briefly, Prime Minister. Tradition has it that he would spend many hours sitting at a particular viewpoint along the lower path from the Blenheim Pavilion. The story goes that Canning sat here under the shelter of an aged oak that predated the first house at Cliveden. That oak fell in the early part of the 21st century, but the view that Canning enjoyed is still popular with today's visitors.

Above Canning's Oak, under which the statesman is said to have sat for hours enjoying the view, fell in 2004. However, the view he loved so lives on

Left George Canning was briefly George IV's Prime Minister in 1827

The War Memorial Garden

William Astor excavated this shady area from the steep slope to create an Italian garden. In 1902 the ground was levelled and paved with mosaic; a water feature was built and cypress trees planted around the perimeter. A 1904 photograph shows the oval shape of the sunken garden, overhung by tall trees.

Some of William Astor's sculptures were placed in this suitably Italianate setting, including a marble screen and some ancient stone and marble columns and capitals.

When war broke out in 1914, Nancy and Waldorf Astor offered facilities for a hospital at Cliveden to the Canadian Red Cross. Cliveden's Italian garden was consecrated in 1917–18 to create a cemetery for those who died in the hospital. The mosaics were taken up and replaced by turf into which were set flat memorial tablets, marking the graves. The 42 burials include those of two Canadian nursing sisters.

The statue opposite the entrance was intended to represent Canada in female form. It was carved and cast in bronze by Australian Sir Bertram MacKennal, who is said to have loosely based the facial features on those of Nancy Astor.

Left Bertram MacKennal's statue in the War Memorial Garden symbolises Canada

Below Looking down the 172 steps of Yew Tree Walk

Octagon Temple and Yew Tree Walk

Above The Octagon Temple was designed as a resting point in a tour of Lord Orkney's pleasure ground

Below right The additions of stained glass and mosaics made the Octagon Temple a fitting resting place for three generations of the Astor family

The Octagon Temple offered a resting and a viewing point in Lord Orkney's pleasure ground. Walkers could enjoy wandering down from the Blenheim Pavilion, along gravel paths running along the top of the cliff, past the House and the Parterre to the Octagon Temple, and down the steep slope of Yew Tree Walk to the river.

Lord Orkney was intent on improving his house and garden, employing the best architects to help him. Giacomo Leoni, at the forefront of the Palladian revival movement, provided designs not only for the Blenheim Pavilion (see page 10) but also for Lord Orkney's last garden building, the Octagon Temple (1735), intended as a temple of peace and, with its 'Prospect Room' in the domed upper storey, a place to enjoy the wide views over the Thames. Below was a little room, cool and grotto-like.

Lord Orkney's temple was altered almost 160 years later by William Astor who, with the help of architect Frank Pearson, turned it into a highly ornate family chapel. Interior walls and ceiling were removed to make a single space, the dome studded with brilliant mosaics depicting the life of Christ and scenes from the Old Testament. The remains of William Astor, his son Waldorf, daughter-in-law Nancy and of their son William are interred here.

The Parterre

Cliveden's extraordinary terrace, more than 360 feet (110 metres) long, at least 26 feet (8 metres) from the ground and generously wide, has distant views over the Thames to the horizon. This grand stage overlooks an equally spectacular scene – Cliveden's unparallelled Parterre.

The Parterre – devised by Lord Orkney as a far plainer feature in 1723 but made glorious by Harriet, Duchess of Sutherland and her Head Gardener, John Fleming – fills a level grass platform that covers over six acres behind the House.

The Duke and Duchess of Sutherland bought Cliveden in 1849 as a country retreat for Harriet to be near her friend, Queen Victoria, at Windsor Castle. Unfortunately the house burnt down soon after the purchase, but was rebuilt by architect Charles Barry, who also put forward designs for a parterre.

However, these were passed over in favour of the ideas of John Fleming, pioneer of

Humble origins
The simple parterre devised by George Hamilton, Earl of Orkney, in 1723–24 was described by him as a 'Quaker parter, for it is very plain'. It was a rectangular lawn flanked by raised walks and a circular bed at the far end, the whole surrounded by a double row of elm trees.

ribbon and carpet bedding, who designed a striking avenue of two sets of eight paired triangular beds.

Gardening on a higher level
Seen from the terrace, these beds, perfectly in scale with the vast area they had to fill, created an innovative pattern, drawing the eye down to the Thames, gleaming silver in the distance. At the far end of the Parterre, Fleming planted the circular bed that survived from Lord Orkney's days.

Fleming's original beds were edged with clipped privet and spruce. The outer beds were filled with seasonal plants – narcissus, jonquils, grape hyacinth, forget-me-nots, campion, anemones, daisies and thousands of tulips in the spring, replaced in the summer by half-hardy annuals such as scarlet pelargoniums, cineraria, love-lies-bleeding and lobelia. Inside the outer beds were grass strips around central beds of shrubby azaleas and rhododendrons, interspersed with tall spires of foxgloves, gladioli and hollyhocks.

At the corners of the triangles were round 'stud' beds filled with roses and bedding plants. In particular Fleming used pansies in vibrant colours, plants that he bred at Cliveden and displayed in great numbers. His use of bedding plants in general and pansies in particular became famous and was copied, becoming standard in many great gardens.

Right The Parterre in summer

The Parterre

Cliveden was acquired by Hugh Lupus (1825–99), Earl Grosvenor, the son-in-law of the Duchess of Sutherland, after her death in 1868. In 1874 the immensely wealthy Earl became the 1st Duke of Westminster. Head Gardener John Fleming retired some time around 1880 but even after his departure, his influence held sway. The Parterre was largely unaltered when William Astor arrived at Cliveden. However, his arrival heralded a significant addition – the Borghese Balustrade.

The Borghese Balustrade

In 1896 William Astor bought the travertine (a form of limestone) marble and brick-tiled balustrade (1618–19) from the Borghese family's villa in Italy. (The Borghese name is prominent in Italian history, being of noble and papal background.) It features carvings of the family's dragon and eagle.

At the far end of the lawn is a copy of William Astor's bronze 'The Rape of Proserpina' (1565) by Vincenzo de' Rossi. The original is on long-term loan to the Victoria and Albert Museum.

Beyond this and down some steps from the Parterre William Astor added another feature to celebrate the view from that spot: the Tortoise Fountain made by Thomas Waldo Story, designer of the Fountain of Love (see page 7). Around it is a miniature version of the Borghese Balustrade. The tortoise motif is from a fountain that was near Story's studio in Rome.

A foreign import

In 2004, a colony of small Mediterranean snails, previously unknown in England, was found living on the Borghese Balustrade. It is thought they were accidentally imported with the Balustrade more than 100 years ago. The snail has a pinky-grey spindle-shaped shell that is only about 11 millimetres long. The snail has no English name but is scientifically called *Papillifera bidens*.

Above left Summer
bedding – ageratums and
pelargoniums

Above centre Spring
bedding – anemones and
narcissus

Above right Spring
bedding – forget-me-nots
and tulips

A platform for entertaining

When Nancy and Waldorf Astor moved in, Cliveden was where they entertained their friends – politicians, writers, philosophers, artists and the celebrities of the day – and they even played host to a monarch. In 1907 King Edward VII came to dinner, re-establishing the 19th-century relationship between Cliveden and Windsor, when the Duchess of Sutherland and Queen Victoria were great friends. In the years before the First World War, guests included Lawrence of Arabia, Rudyard Kipling, Winston Churchill and Charlie Chaplin. They would gather in the great rooms opening on to the terrace, with a view of the celebrated Parterre.

Progressive planting

With resources reduced in the interwar years, the planting of the Parterre was simplified. Shrubs of the same variety were displayed within the clipped box hedges. This type of planting persisted until 2010 when the National Trust reverted to John Fleming's mid-19th-century bedding style.

Central beds are filled in summer with plants such as azaleas which are underplanted with gladioli. In the outer beds rows of plants such as red pelargoniums, white alyssum and blue lobelia make a multi-coloured thread. In spring each of the 16 beds is filled with 600 bulbs and glows with massed pansies and primulas.

The House and Forecourt

The Grand Avenue, flanked by lawns and a row of tall lime trees, sweeps to the Forecourt which, in turn, leads to the *cour d'honneur*, or large inner courtyard, at the main entrance to the House.

The Forecourt is laid to two large lawns, on which stand two ancient mulberry trees. The walls behind each lawn, thickly clad in climbing plants, shelter deep herbaceous borders. The borders were first laid out by Norah Lindsay, who was employed by Nancy and Waldorf Astor on an annual retainer of £100. She had the borders edged with stone paving to ensure that the lawns could be mowed with ease. She filled the beds with tall delphiniums, lupins, campanula, phlox and pyrethrum, setting off the lower-growing clumps of stachys, thrift, dianthus, centranthus, saxifrage and other perennials.

They were redesigned in 1968 by Graham Stuart Thomas, giving brilliant and contrasting colour for most of the year. As you enter the Forecourt via the 18th-century yew hedge, you'll see that the border on the right, the western side, is planted with drifts of cool mauves, blues, creams and white. On your left the plantings are 'hot', based on strong yellows with reds and oranges, scarlets and deep pinks. These lavish borders now stand as a tribute to Graham Stuart Thomas, one of the 20th century's great plantsmen and the National Trust's Gardens Advisor during the 1960s and '70s.

Opposite above The Italianate Clock Tower, built in 1861, is actually a water tower supplying the House

Opposite below The Grand Avenue is flanked by ancient Roman sarcophagi collected by William Astor; this 3rd-century Roman sarcophagus is from the Villa Borghese

Left The 'hot' colours in one of the great herbaceous borders flanking the Forecourt lawn

A Latin lesson

The inscription in the frieze that runs around all four sides of the House was provided by W. E. Gladstone, four-times Prime Minister between 1868 and 1894, and offers a useful summary of the complex architectural history of Cliveden House.

North front: AEDIFICATA FUNDAMENTIS A GEO VILLIERS BUCKINGHAMIAE DUCE OLIM LOCATIS REGE CAROLO SECONDO Built on the foundations laid by George Villiers, Duke of Buckingham in the reign of Charles II

South front: INSTAURATA DOMM II PRIUS IBIDEM IGNE ABSUMPTIS A GEO DUCE SUTHERLANDIAE ET HENRIETTA UXORE Established by George, Duke of Sutherland and his wife Harriet after the second house formerly on the same site had been destroyed by fire

East front: EXSTRUCTA A.D. MDCCCLI ANNUM IAM XIV DEO AUSP REGNANTE VICTORIA Constructed in the year 1851, the 14th year of Victoria's glorious reign

West front: POSTIA INGENIO OPERA CONSILIO CAROLI BARRY ARCHIT. A MDCCCLI The work accomplished by the brilliant plan of the architect Charles Barry in 1851

The ornate dovecote (1869) marking the end of the eastern border and the spectacular gilded 100-foot (30-metre) Clock Tower (1861) on the western side – which is in fact a well-disguised and still operational water tower – were the work of architect Henry Clutton. A statue of the Spirit of Liberty stands lightly atop the tower which has a half-open spiral staircase built into its south face.

Eight richly carved marble Roman sarcophagi lie at the north of the Forecourt. They were placed here by William Astor at the end of the 19th century. Some are almost 2,000 years old.

The Maze

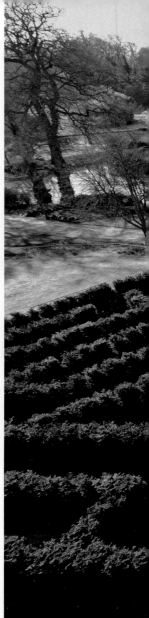

A paper sketch of a cleverly conceived maze was speedily translated into the real thing by the army of gardeners and bottomless wallet of multi-millionaire William Astor. He sketched the layout for a yew maze in 1893, the same year he made Cliveden his country mansion, and work began in 1894.

The Maze, which covers one third of an acre, is historically important, marking, as it did, a new and lavish phase in the design of these gardens which had already been established for 200 years when William Astor bought the estate. Even when set against the Water Garden, Long Garden and the ancient statues and sarcophagi, William Astor's 'labyrinth' was one of the most spectacular features that he introduced.

By the 1950s, the once perfectly maintained maze was a thing of the past, largely dug out and all but forgotten. Half a century later, the plan for the maze, drawn on a sheet of writing paper, was discovered in the Cliveden archives and the decision was made to reinstate it.

> 'In The Captain's Field the Labyrinth was designed by me in 1893 and laid out by Sanders.'
>
> William Astor, 1905

Amazing facts
The new Maze was opened in April 2011 by gardening broadcaster and writer Alan Titchmarsh in the presence of the 4th Viscount Astor, great-grandson of William Astor. The project took two years from start to finish, used 1,100 semi-mature yew trees and 120 tonnes of gravel for the 547 yards (500 metres) of pathways. Many of the trees have been donated by supporters.

A puzzling restoration
It was not possible to re-create the maze in its original position, but a faithful copy of the original opened close to that spot in 2011. The curving design, complex shape and detailed planting of the new Maze made this restoration one of the most technically challenging ever undertaken by the National Trust.

Cliveden's gardeners pegged out the paths before planting 10-year-old yew trees, which were already six feet (two metres) tall, so that

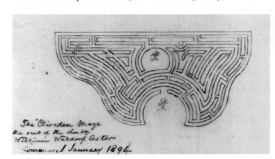

Above The Maze is a faithful copy of William Astor's design (see left)

the Maze would prove a real puzzle right from the start. The trees were planted when they were tall enough to obscure sight of the exit, and short-cuts through the yews are prevented by railings that line the winding paths, protecting the hedges.

Now, as visitors test the twists and turns of the maze, entering through magnificent iron gates, designed and hand-forged by a local craftsman, a maze-keeper counts them in and out, to make sure that no-one is lost along the way.

The Water Garden

When William Astor bought Cliveden in 1893, one of his first instructions besides the creation of the maze was to enlarge the small duck pond in the so-called 'Captain's Field', so that it could be used for skating. An island was created in the lake, later connected to the surrounding land by two bridges.

What is now the Water Garden was planned by William Astor as part of his major redesign of the gardens. By the turn of the century he had developed this area into a garden that was oriental in character. This effect was achieved through the use of water, rocks and a six-sided Chinese pagoda made for the 1867 Paris Exposition Universelle, that William Astor bought from the sale of the Bagatelle, the Marquess of Hertford's villa near Paris in 1900. He referred to this new area as the 'Japanese Garden'.

By 1913, when Nancy and Waldorf Astor were living at Cliveden, the lake had been enlarged, stepping stones added and the oriental theme enhanced with the planting of Japanese cherries, bamboo and great drifts of irises.

A place of contemplation

This was a time of huge interest in all things Japanese. That said, the design at Cliveden was oriental in character rather than specifically Japanese. It followed current fashion, without taking the purist line followed by many other Edwardian gardeners.

By the 1930s the area was known as the Water Garden. An article published in a 1930 edition of *Country Life* magazine enthused about the Cliveden Water Garden, praising this 'modern development in gardening where the formal has no place, the beauty and charm of the garden picture depending on the natural use of water and the free disposition of the plant material to enhance the landscape setting'. The writer tells us that plants included water lilies, hostas, many primulas, grasses (including *Miscanthus sinensis*), flowering rush,

drifts of astilbes, calthas and mimulus, *Cotoneaster horizontalis*, azaleas, acers and tree paeonies, loosestrife, great clumps of rhubarb-like *Gunnera manicata* and leafy bergenias.

Since the mid-1960s the National Trust has created a series of island planting beds and borders to provide a more varied landscape within the Water Garden. Many of these beds have recently been refined and revamped. Oriental plants, such as ginkgo, magnolias and iris, have been added to the garden to both enhance and extend the seasonal interest whilst also strengthening the original garden design conceived by William Astor. The autumnal colours of trees such as liquidamber are particularly stunning when reflected in the water.

Opposite The Water Garden has foliage to enjoy in all seasons

Below The pagoda was made for the Paris Exposition Universelle of 1867 and bought by William Astor in 1900 to provide a centrepiece for his oriental-inspired garden

Above The golden dragon atop the Chinese Pagoda

Into the Woods

The Hanging Woods at Cliveden were famous long before a house was built on the land behind them. In the years since the Duke of Buckingham constructed his mansion here in the late 17th century, successive owners have planted trees on the estate, laid paths and designed avenues and vistas to take in the many wonderful views.

The Hanging Woods lining the steep cliffs above the Thames on the western side of the estate have long been admired. The 1860 *Handbook for Travellers in Bucks, Berks and Oxfordshire* is effusive in their praise: 'Cliefden runs along the summit of a lofty ridge which overhangs the river. The outline of this ridge is broken in the most agreeable way; the steep bank is clothed with luxuriant foliage, forming a hanging wood of great beauty…. These exquisite woods abound in magnificent primeval yew trees, which hang from the chalk cliffs.'

Much of the woodland and most of the paths were laid out by Lord Orkney in the early 18th century. Successive owners have

restocked the woodland, while the National Trust, which took over the care of the grounds in 1966, has restored and cleared the paths and replanted many of those trees lost in the storms of the late 20th century.

High points in the woods

Today's visitor may spend the best part of a day exploring several miles of Cliveden's woods, taking the riverside walk to link, by way of a zigzag path, with the Duke's Seat, where the great statue of the Duke of Sutherland stands, having been removed from the head of the Grand Avenue in 1896. Nearby is a massive section of a giant redwood (*Sequoia gigantea*), brought here in 1897 by William Astor from California. The path carries on south from the Duke's Seat to a high point overlooking the river with panoramic views over the Berkshire countryside. Green Drive, a ride created by the Orkney family in the early 18th century, runs for more than a mile along the eastern side of the estate, joining other walks and rides through the woods.

Opposite above The Hanging Woods above the River Thames at Cliveden, bearing the colours of autumn

Opposite below The south front of Cliveden, viewed from the Duke's Seat

Below The Bluebell Woods

Cliveden Reach and Spring Cottage

Left Spring Cottage by the Thames

Opposite Cliveden ferry, with Ferry Cottage beyond; photograph by Henry Taunt, *c*.1883

Cliveden Reach, the two-mile stretch of the Thames winding beneath the high ground on which the House stands, is often called the most beautiful part of the river. Here the Duchess of Sutherland commissioned George Devey in the late 1850s to build three cottages and a boat house in a rustic style using timber, brick and local tiles.

Devey also extended and adapted the existing Spring Cottage, named for the natural springs that flowed nearby. The cottage, set underneath the Hanging Woods, was originally built for the 4th Countess of Orkney in 1799. She extended it 14 years later, employing architect Peter Nicholson to create a domed gothic dining room so that she could entertain her well-to-do visitors – some of whom would arrive by boat from Windsor Castle – in a romantically rustic setting, but also in comfort.

One notable visitor who would make the journey up the Thames from Windsor was Queen Victoria. Harriet, Duchess of Sutherland, had enormous influence at court, being Mistress of the Robes and a great friend to Queen Victoria. When Victoria's beloved husband, Albert, died in 1861, Harriet was the person to whom she clung for support.

The riverside walk takes you behind the cottage (which is not open to visitors) and continues southwards. You can return by way of the woods on the eastern side of the estate or turn back to take the steeper route up the 172 steps of Yew Tree Walk.

Scandal at Cliveden

Spring Cottage achieved notoriety in the early 1960s when osteopath Dr Stephen Ward invited his friends, call-girls Christine Keeler and Mandy Rice-Davies, there to share his weekend retreat. Up at the House the women, frolicking in the swimming pool, happened to catch the attention of John Profumo, Secretary of State for War, and thus began the scandal that damaged the Macmillan government and ended Profumo's political career.

Cliveden Centre Stage

Cliveden, evocative of a past interwoven with more than 300 years of English history, continues to attract people eager to experience its unique atmosphere. Visitors today may walk the paths, share the views and enjoy the gardens once frequented by kings and queens, titled and wealthy families, distinguished soldiers, influential politicians, writers, thinkers and artists.

Below Visitors in the Cockerell Pavilion at the western end of the terrace overlooking the Parterre

artistic society. Guests from Lloyd George, Herbert Henry Asquith, Anthony Eden, Winston Churchill and Neville Chamberlain to Sylvia Pankhurst, George Bernard Shaw, Henry Ford, Gandhi, Amy Johnson and Charlie Chaplin were invited to enjoy the lavish hospitality of the House and the beauty of the gardens.

A wider public became aware of Cliveden in 1963 after John Profumo, Secretary of State for War in the Macmillan government, met call-girl Christine Keeler here, when he was a guest of the 3rd Lord Astor. Profumo's brief affair with Keeler, who was also involved with Soviet naval attaché Evegeny Ivanov, raised fears about national security.

Left Nancy Astor with George Bernard Shaw on the terrace

Left John Profumo was Secretary of State for War when he began an affair with Christine Keeler in 1961

Below Christine Keeler and her friend Mandy Rice-Davies

Since it was built high above the Thames in the second half of the 17th century, Cliveden has been a powerhouse – a place visited by royalty and the politically influential. Its first owner, the Duke of Buckingham, was brought up with the children of Charles I, and was instrumental in the restoration of Charles II in 1660, a move that brought him the wealth to build this great house.

Lord Orkney, the next owner, and his wife, Elizabeth Villiers, a one-time mistress of William III, hosted both George I and George II at Cliveden, while their successors the Sutherland family, among the wealthiest in the land, were often visited by Queen Victoria.

However it was during the tenure of Nancy and Waldorf Astor that Cliveden became the glamorous centre of political, literary and

To the future

Cliveden continues to refresh and impress as much as its first owners intended

Cliveden was presented to the National Trust in 1942 by Waldorf Astor with a Memorandum of Wishes. In the memorandum he expressed a wish for the House to be used for 'a better understanding between the English-speaking world'.

The Astors continued to live here until the death of William, the 3rd Lord Astor, in 1966. The National Trust took over the running of the estate, letting the House to Stanford University of California for their English educational programmes, fulfilling Lord Astor's wishes. When the university's agreement ran out in the mid-1980s, the Trust undertook major repairs to the House, before leasing it to a hotel company who, in turn, undertook refurbishment of the interiors with the guidance of Trust experts.

The House, apart from a few rooms open briefly during the week, is not open to the public, but the gardens, woods and riverside – which cover 376 acres (156 hectares) – have been opened with an ongoing programme of restoration and replanting since 1966. This includes re-creating seasonal bedding on the Parterre, designing colourful displays for the Long Garden and re-creating the Maze.

Successive owners have preserved garden designs and early planting plans, enabling the Trust to maintain the spirit of Cliveden which has delighted, enchanted and entertained so many over the course of 350 years, and will continue to do so for many more.